Extraordinary Life Lessons from Ordinary Christian Women

Extraordinary Life Lessons from Ordinary Christian Women

STORIES OF ENCOURAGEMENT

God bless you for your faithfulness!
Kathy Eberly
Lam. 3:22-23
P. 75

Kathy Eberly

Copyright © 2009 by Kathy Eberly.

Library of Congress Control Number: 2009911894
ISBN: Hardcover   978-1-4415-9841-7
             Softcover   978-1-4415-9840-0
             Ebook   978-1-4415-9842-4

All rights reserved. No part of this book may be reproduced or transmitted in any form or by any means, electronic or mechanical, including photocopying, recording, or by any information storage and retrieval system, without permission in writing from the copyright owner.

This book was printed in the United States of America.

To order additional copies of this book, contact:
Xlibris Corporation
1-888-795-4274
www.Xlibris.com
Orders@Xlibris.com
70516

CONTENTS

WHO AM I AND WHY AM I DOING THIS?..................... 9
IMPROVISING CREATORS 13
SELF EDUCATION-STRIVING TO LEARN 23
SURVIVAL-KEEPING IT TOGETHER THOUGH YOU FEEL LIKE YOU'RE LOSING IT 29
HOSPITALITY-THAT FORGOTTEN ART 41
LIFE LESSONS IN THE WORKPLACE......................... 53
HAPPILLY EVER SINGLE 63
ENCOURAGERS ALONG THE WAY 73
SOMETIMES IT'S HARD TO STAND BY YOUR MAN 79
SHORT TERM FRIENDSHIPS THAT LAST FOREVER...... 87
STANDING BY MY MAN ALL THE WAY 97
LORD, IT'S HARD TO BE HUMBLE 103
THINGS DIDN'T GO THE WAY I PLANNED THEM 109

DEDICATION

This book is dedicated to my mother, Jan who has encouraged me, for my grandmothers Myrtle and Marion for their strong testimony and perseverance. To Wendy who encouraged me to go forward with this project; to my support team: Barb, Debbie, Sue, and Kathy for being there for me; and especially to my husband Dale for all of his support in this venture.

WHO AM I AND WHY AM I DOING THIS?

"I have learned in whatever state I am to be content," Phillipians 4:11b

I'm an ordinary woman. I don't look too spectacular, I exercise but I'm still trying to get those bulges under control. My face contains lines of many years on Earth. I long ago stopped wearing make-up because I found it tediously repetitive and hard to keep up with; don't get me wrong, occasionally I will put on some eye shadow and lipstick to "Paint the Old Barn", but my husband likes me as I am, for which I have been grateful. I don't see myself as having accomplished anything too noteworthy. I now feel okay with where I am in life, but it took me a LONG, LONG time to get to this point. I turned 50 this year. YEAH! A lot of women I know grimace each year when they have birthdays but not me.

This year I embraced my aging with a new zest; although there are days that I get up and I find that I can't move like I did in my early 20's. It seems like the older I get the more memories I try to hold on to.

I love to tell stories. I feel like I have a million of them inside of me, each one waiting to be told whether to strangers or to family, each story and each person represents a part of my life that I need to remember and each one tells a lesson.

Not too long ago I stood at a funeral where I saw many people that had at one point or another in my life had impacted me in a great way. I had waited for many years to share the gratitude that I felt for each person and I found myself telling each person my favorite memory and their profoundness in my otherwise ordinary life. Tears welled in their eyes when I gave them thanks and they thanked me for telling them.

I want to share some of the lessons I have learned from the special people I have met along the way. Thank you for taking time out of your life to share my life. I hope that somehow these stories help bless you as well.

IMPROVISING CREATORS

Proverbs 31 talks quite a bit about the virtuous woman. Solomon speaks about a woman who looks after the needs of her own household as being blessed. To me the women in this section are the epitome of improvisation.

MYRTLE

Myrtle was born in 1917 to a poor but caring family in Central Wisconsin. As the only daughter of four children, Myrtle learned early and quickly how to make a meal for her family and also how to design clothing out of nothing. She completed six years of elementary education and never had the opportunity to go further, but she had a desire to learn by watching her grandmother and mother to keep a home tidy

Although Myrtle had little self-confidence, she was talented beyond measure. She was able to construct a lovely fashion creation by looking at a picture in a magazine or in a catalog. She designed many lovely clothes for her entire family. She could make anything from under garments to suits for her husband and the clothes were sturdy and stood up over time.

Not only was Myrtle talented in fashion; she was also an excellent cook. She concocted many tasty dishes for her family from scratch and even developed many tasty diabetic meals. She had her own that was about ½ acre in size and continued growing her food long into her 70's. This incredible woman made food from scratch even after she was diagnosed with colon cancer; when a craving enticed her to can home made chili sauce. She made the precious sauce just two weeks before succumbing to the cancer that took her life. The chili sauce and her full cupboards of home canned meats and soups and the like were a constant reminder for several months after Myrtle's passing of Myrtle's resourceful and caring attitude. It was important to her that her husband still be fed and cared for long after she was gone.

As much as Myrtle loved sewing and cooking, however, it was her great love for God that kept her going through those years. She took to heart the great verse "My God shall supply all your needs according to His riches in Christ Jesus." In her own poem, "My Kitchen", Myrtle shares with pride those things that were closest to her heart.

MY KITCHEN

I love my kitchen because it is mine.
I learned to cook when I was nine.

I love to plan my own meal
Cook and bake and potatoes peel.
I love to bake bread, rolls and pie
I guess I'll love to do it until I die.

I love to be boss in my kitchen you see.
I love to do it because it belongs to me.
I don't tell others in their kitchen what to do.
Because that kitchen belongs to you.

I help with the dishes most places I go.
And lend a hand to be helpful you know.
I'm not as helpful as I used to be.
Because I'm a little older you see.

I don't make many cold lunches and such
Because good cooked meals mean so much.
Vegetables, potatoes, meat and gravy too.
Pudding, cake or rolls for dessert will do.

Spiritual food means the most to me.
It shows the way you see.
Jesus died on the cross for me
And someday with Jesus in Heaven I'll be.

God is the eternal improviser. He can take someone who feels as though they are nothing and makes them into a vessel that He can use for His glory.

BRENDA

Along the same line of improvisation I think of Brenda. She married my brother a few years back and is every bit the Proverbs 31 woman in my eyes. I cannot begin to do the justice that she deserves but I would like to highlight just a few of her virtues.

When Brenda married my brother she was an elementary school teacher in a Christian school and taught first graders. I could only imagine what a great teacher she was to her students and how much they must have missed their teacher when she began her family. Brenda is a wonderful mother. From the time she had her very first baby until the present time, she has insisted on taking care of her own children and not palming them off on sitters to enjoy her career. She felt that her career was her children and she has taken that further. With each child that she has given birth to and there have been six, she has treated each one like they are special and not one of her children is unwanted. She home schooled her children until recently with the same tenderness that she taught her classrooms so long ago. Contrast that with many parents who value the career above their children. Brenda sews many of her children's clothes and also prepares all of their meals, usually preparing the food from scratch. She wants to make sure that each person who enters the home is well fed. On each family member's birthday, she creates a beautiful cake that is as special as the family member that she bakes it for.

Whenever I go to see my brother and Brenda, I am amazed at her hospitality. Some time ago; our mother was hospitalized in Rochester, and Brenda opened up her home to my two sons, my daughter, another brother and my father. She made sure we were comfortable in the beds as well as made sure that we were all satisfied from hunger.

A lot of people make a lot of different comments about parenting; but in my opinion, parents who love their children, take care of their children without complaining are good parents that should not be belittled. They are doing as God has commanded; they are being fruitful and multiplying and they are raising their children to love the Savior.

I am proud that my brother was so wise and careful in his choice of a life partner. May we raise our children to wisely seek God's face in choosing his life's partner.

DOROTHY

God has blessed me with all kinds of creative women in my life and my life has been extremely blessed by my great Aunt Dorothy. Dorothy has been one of the most creative women I have known. For as long as I have known her, Dorothy's seamstress ability has astounded me. When my mother married my father, Aunt Dorothy made my mother's wedding dress and hand covered over 50 buttons on the dress and hand sewed them on. I was so blessed to be able to wear the same dress down the aisle when I married years later.

The thing that is so amazing is that my Aunt Dorothy has had poor vision for years. She had been badly injured years before, but amazingly up until the past couple of years still continued to sew baby quilts for babies in her church and she has also for many years sewed a complete wardrobe for her daughter. Though she is now 89 and closer to spending her eternity with her savior, she has left a legacy with the beautiful creations she has made.

COLLEEN

A while back I met a very special woman in my church. Colleen had been a wedding coordinator in our church for several years. I approached Colleen about my daughter's wedding and she graciously offered to help me. I dearly wanted to make my daughter's wedding a beautiful one but I also knew that as a single mom my resources were limited. From the attractive favors to the lovely flowers, Colleen's hand was seen in her handiwork. Colleen stayed up late with me the night before my daughter's wedding making the real bouquets and corsages that we had chosen to create. She also helped me to coordinate her wedding reception; a simple but elegant affair.

Colleen's gift is definitely creativity. She is active in most of the functions in her current church in the event planning, etc. I don't think I could have managed such a beautiful wedding had it not been for her.

TAMMY

Tammy was only 17 years old when I met her the first time and she entered my family. She had never cooked or sewn or done many domestic items. In short order however, Tammy soon learned those skills. She spent many years when things were tight sewing clothes for her children, preparing her own meals from scratch. I can still taste her homemade pizza. It rivals the major pizza chains. Tammy home schooled her children until they entered high school and junior high school. Not too long ago I noticed that Tammy had taken on a new craft. She is now designing and making beautiful one of a kind jewelry. They are such gorgeous creations that she is in great demand. In addition to her regular job in an office, Tammy is now making and designing many works of art.

God has blessed Tammy and my brother with blessings in many ways, Tammy still uses the same skills that she used 28 years ago.

As I finish this section about women who are improvisers, I encourage you to think of women that you know who are Proverbs 31 women who look to the needs of their households and take care of their families.

Can you think of someone in your life who you think of is a great improviser? Write their story here.

SELF EDUCATION-STRIVING TO LEARN

"My children will enjoy the works of their hand." Isaiah 65:22

I have always thirsted for knowledge. From the time I was a small girl I have enjoyed reading and learning about things I didn't know. The woman in this section is a wonderful example of a woman who desires to know truth.

MARGARET

Margaret was one of six children brought up by her single mother in an era where divorce was taboo. In the 1800's, a woman's education wasn't considered as much as important as it is these days. So, like many others, Margaret did not complete her education. This was because she was needed at home.

So, Margaret decided to teach herself the things that were important. To increase her word power, she often was found perusing the "word power" section in the Reader's Digest issues to increase her vocabulary. It became a game to her to see just which words she knew and which ones would enhance her life.

She was also well read. Reading was a passion to Margaret and she passed that passion on to her children, grandchildren and great grandchildren. She was always reading about medical procedures and medicines. Margaret had chronic migraine headaches so she was always studying to see if there were new treatments on the horizon. Although she only lived to be 67, Margaret left a strong heritage of a thirst for knowledge. How astounded she would be if she could see today's technology and how advanced medicine is in this time.

God's word tells us that we are to "Get wisdom, get understanding, guard her and she will serve you well." How much more ahead of her time was this beautiful woman who treasured knowledge both spiritually and physically. If she could talk today, she would emphatically share these principles.

God's word says much about education and the importance of it. Can you think of someone who has or had a thirst for knowledge in your life? How did they impact you and your thirst for knowledge?

SURVIVAL-KEEPING IT TOGETHER THOUGH YOU FEEL LIKE YOU'RE LOSING IT

"Do not forsake your mother's teaching".
Proverbs 1:8

Years ago I heard a humorous song about being a survivor by a well-known Christian couple. I chuckled as I heard all of the things that go on in a young mother's life. I remember myself that I wondered if I would ever survive those difficult days from babyhood, to toddler, to teens and then adulthood. Though the words of the song are humorous, the women in this section are survivors in their own right. I am amazed at how God helps some women survive what I would think are insurmountable challenges.

TILLIE

Imagine being abandoned by your husband and being left with several children and having to raise them by yourself. This sounds like the norm for this day and age, but for the 1800's, it was uncommon. Tillie set out to teach her children the techniques to survival that she could with the skills that she had, often not having enough money to make ends meet.

Not to be deterred, however, Tillie decided to take her former spouse to task for not paying his proper amount in child support, so, she hitch-hiked all the way across Wisconsin to his home to demand the money that she so desperately needed for her family. I can only imagine his surprise when he saw his former spouse actually come looking for him. How much of an advocate she would be today with forgotten single mothers and the illusive fathers of their children. She would definitely leave no stone unturned in searching and retrieving necessary funds.

MAGDELINA

When I think of survivors, I without a doubt think of Magdelina. Magdelina was from Liberia. In the early 80's she seemingly had it all. But in an instant, her life changed forever. As many people know, there has been a civil war in Liberia since the late 1980's. Magdelina's husband was a prominent official in the community. Magdelina and her husband and their family lived in luxury. She had many material items at her disposal.

Magdelina speaks candidly about her experience of a neighbor taking her three-month old twins for safekeeping and she talks about fleeing to what should have been a safe place for herself and her family. She had no idea what would ensue following that event or even what would become of her babies. She and her family were kept in internment camps for several years until when it appeared that she and her husband would be re-united and travel to America.

During her time of exile, Magdelina helped to start an orphanage for the children that were abandoned during the ordeal.

Eventually, she and two of her children left their family behind and traveled with another family to America under events that can only be described as God incidence not coincidence. The plan was that Magdelina and her husband would meet at a future time in America with hopes that their family would be reunited there.

Unfortunately, after arriving in America, Magdelina learned that she was expecting another child. It was a bittersweet time for her and I often wonder how she was able to cope knowing that she was separated from the rest of her family and yet she was bringing a new child into the world. To begin a new life in America without her husband to many women would have been unthinkable and she continued to pray for his safe return to her.

This was a difficult time for this courageous woman, and then she heard the unthinkable. Her husband and many family members had been killed. The tragedy was overwhelming to her. How could God allow this to happen to her and why? Still, Magdelina clung to the hope that God loved her and would guide her.

Unfortunately bad things do happen to good people and there was more tragedy in store for her; this time, grief engulfed this precious woman. Her health continued to fail her: diabetes, arthritis, many other ailments plagued her.

It was at this point that I learned of Magdelina through my pastor's wife. This dear lady had been pushed to her limits and yet, she somehow realized that God did care for her and that He knew what was best. She says that despite her trials she knows He cares for her. He has seen her gain some of her strength back and He alone is whom she depends on for getting her through the days when she feels she cannot go on.

Since I began to write this there have been many changes in Magdelina's life. Although at this time she is still unable to work, she has continued her orphanage ministry by collecting clothing and other needs for the orphanage that she began in Liberia. She collects necessities for the orphans and ships them to the orphanage herself with no church sponsorship. She has gone back to Liberia, only this time as a humanitarian but also, surprisingly to those of us who knew her she remarried a school chum and has moved away. She is happy to be involved in the Lord's work. Magdelina tells everyone who asks, "Everybody says that I am like Job, but I am not, Job was stronger." God is faithful. I am reminded of the verse in Romans 8:28 that says "For all things work together for good to them that are called according to His purpose."

JAN

Jan was born in Oregon at the end of World War II. She often jokes that she was a war baby and good parts were hard to find. This special lady deserves to have her story shared as well. Jan's parents moved to central Wisconsin when she turned three years old. As far back as she can remember, she suffered migraines and was sickly. Jan's parent's were poor and were not able to afford medical or dental care and often times she went without medical attention because of this. Jan was a victim of familial abuse that led to a series of unexpected incidents which changed the course of her life forever. It began with an unexpected pregnancy after a rape at the age of 15.

Silently and by herself she carried this burden alone until the problem could no longer be concealed just two weeks after her 16th birthday. This began a series of health complications that would plague her for years. Jan kept the small newborn though odds were against her.

At the age of 18, she moved away to Minneapolis where she was told that jobs were plentiful so that she could afford to raise her child alone. It was there she met a young man who seemed to adore her child and her and she married him after knowing him for a few months. Within their first year of marriage, Jan and her husband had a son who they felt would be a companion for her daughter and then followed more pregnancies and miscarriages (four in all) and subsequent female problems and other surgeries that were to follow.

Though Jan had to drop out of high school, she elected to take her GED. Jan describes that day in an amusing tone. She sat down to take the test and finished it in record time, bringing the test back to the administrator, "That was a tough one," she recalls saying. "Well didn't you take the class before the test?" the testing official asked. Jan shook her head. She hadn't known. When the results came back she was amazed that she had only missed a couple of questions.

In her early 30's, Jan encountered the beginning of many back surgeries that she would endure. Still, Jan managed to keep cheerful and continued to raise her children despite the fact that she was ill a great deal of the time.

After her last son left home, Jan decided to embark on a new career in medicine. She was talented enough that she could have become a doctor but she opted to become a medical assistant, to work with a doctor in a professional setting. Unfortunately, her health did not cooperate with her and she was forced to discontinue her external training and had to wait several years before she could take her certification exam and to procure a position with a prominent plastic surgeon in the Minneapolis area. She enjoyed her job immensely but continued to have other health problems.

Jan is no longer working (she has had neurological surgery and heart surgery that impairs her ability to work, and complete the tasks that she used to), she has not given up the hope that God is with her and will not leave her or forsake her.

NANCY

Nancy grew up in rural Minnesota. She was youngest of six children. She would be the first to tell you that her life was anything but a picnic. As the youngest you would think that this young lady would be the favored of the bunch, but I learned that Nancy's life was anything but favorable. Her life was filled with abuse.

When she was 17, she rebelled. She left home and moved to the Minneapolis area to get a job working with a local business as a telephone operator. Nancy had been somewhat wild, people would say. She enjoyed the freedom that being away from her parents afforded. She was very young, but she met a young man who was being released from a tour of duty in the army and in no time at all, she realized she was pregnant. Nancy was not really prepared for the responsibility of being a wife and mother; nevertheless, she married her baby's father and gave birth a few months later to her daughter. Life for the young couple was anything but easy, although the two tried to make the marriage work. Within a year after their first daughter was born, a second daughter was born. She was a beautiful child and it appeared that all would go well as it had with her previous baby.

Two weeks into the baby's life, the baby died of sudden infant death syndrome. Nancy and her young husband were unprepared for the loss that happened to them. Although, as a youngster, Nancy had lost her brother, it was not the same as losing your own child. The couple bore another child, a son after a time but the marriage was beyond repair. Subsequently, the couple divorced. Nancy's husband committed suicide. Nancy continually searched for the love that she felt she had not received earlier in life.

Nancy remarried, but that marriage also ended in divorce.

A while after this Nancy discovered that she had breast cancer. Nancy learned much during this ordeal. She also remembered her origin. She realized that she had sinned and needed a savior. She had been brought up in Sunday school and knew the right way. Nancy's life turned around. While she did not heal from the cancer, she healed her relationship with God and with many of her family members. She faced many of her inner demons that tormented her. Nancy was a survivor, she had faced the loss of a close sibling, had survived her child's death, had made it through two divorces and a challenging third marriage, but when she died, she was truly free in Christ. God gives second and sometimes third chances and this is evidenced by this story. He gave Nancy every chance to draw herself to Him and she is now with Him forever.

Sometimes survivors keep carrying on with trust in the Lord, which is what he would have us do. It is so hard. In my own life I know that I have had many trials and sometimes I feel that it's a miracle I made it through and think that I am well on my way only to find that there is another monkey wrench thrown into my plans. Of course God has other ideas than me.

When I began this chapter I thought of people who handled their situations with such a positive step that I was encouraged by their stories. But then I realized that there are two sides to the story.

I caught sight of the attractive older woman who walked into an event in Chicago at a prestigious hotel. I could tell that her life had perhaps not been the easiest. She wore expensive rings on each finger and to the average outsider a person might think this woman had it all; nothing could have been further from the truth.

All too quickly, "**CHRIS**" I will call her began to share about her life. "My mother never wanted me," she said, "She tried to abort me. She hated me". I instantly felt sad for this woman in her late 60's that she had never felt her mother's love. In the days that she was born, abortion was not legal and therefore, her mother had gone to an illegal abortionist. The procedure obviously had not worked and produced many future health problems for the woman.

Consequently, Chris's mother let her fury be known to the child as she grew up and also never had any more siblings. Chris's father seemed to regard her mother with anger at what she had attempted to do and thus began the battle between Chris's parents. Chris always knew that her father loved her, but her mother totally ignored her. In desperate attempts to find the love that she needed, Chris turned to men to try to ease her pain. Unfortunately, Chris discovered that this did not work either.

Chris confided in me that she had one son whom she loved more than words could tell but that they were estranged because of the choice he had made as his wife; he would not even speak to her. She told me that her present husband was a doctor but he was an alcoholic. He psychologist had told her that she had a giant hole in her heart and nothing would ever fill it. I wanted to tell her that the person had told her a lie. That Christ could fill her heart and He alone could bring her joy. Unfortunately I missed the opportunity and Chris is still searching for someone or something to fill her life and unless she finds the Lord and learns to trust Him, she will continue to have a giant-sized hole in her heart.

Survival is the wonderful ability to get through the tough stuff in life and move on. Are you or any others in your life survivors? Please write them down and praise God for those people in your life.

HOSPITALITY-THAT FORGOTTEN ART

"The Lord is my strength and my song; He has become my salvation." Exodus 15:2.

Hospitality seems to have become a forgotten art in our busy daily lives; although there are many examples of hospitality mentioned in the Bible. Mary and Martha are the first to come to my mind. They made our Lord Jesus comfortable and welcomed Him into their home. The Shunamite woman allowed Elisha to have respite during the time of famine. Praise God for the woman who still takes the time to make people feel welcome in an otherwise scary environment. These ladies make my list for the most kind, hospitable ladies that I know.

MARLYS

To anyone who knows Marlys knows that she is hospitable to a fault. The very first time I met Marlys she invited me into her home, ushered me into her daughter's room (I was nine years old) and I began a life long friendship and fellowship with this dear woman and her whole family. The time was a tumultuous one for my family and I, yet Marlys just seemed to know what to do to help. Perhaps this is also what is called a servant heart. Marlys attended our church but she also had known my father since they had gone to school together. From the first time I met Marlys I knew that I had a second mom for life.

Shortly after being re-introduced to Maryls my mother went into the hospital for major surgery. Even though Marlys had five children of her own she took in my three brothers and I for at least three weeks while my mother recovered. This was not just a one-time thing for Marlys to do. She often took in troubled teens that were having problems at home. She became confidante to lonely teenage girls and boys who had no one to talk to. She assisted single moms who didn't know how to mother. She practices what she preaches believing that loving one another is one of God's greatest commandments. To this day if you go by Marlys's home she will usher you into her home with the same zest as she had 30 years ago. Though physically she is more delicate than then she once was, she is such an encouragement to talk with and will also keep you well fed, if you let her.

JANIS-A TEENAGER FOR ALL SEASONS

When I was 15, my parents moved out of the larger city that we lived in to a rural area about 12 miles from where we lived. I was a sophomore in high school and extremely shy. I had left a school of 2500 kids to attend this smaller school. It was with great anticipation yet fear that I stepped onto the bus that first day. It was on that bus that I saw Janis for the first time. She was a year ahead of me I was to learn. I can still see her friendly face and her pleasant tone as she welcomed me to the school. "You are going to love this school," she told me, "there is so much to do. Are you in choir? I just got into concert choir and I love it." She hastened to include me in the events of the school. Now at that time, our school was under construction and we were having split shifts so we were out of school by noon each day. Janis went on to tell me that she was one of the new football cheerleaders (I was in awe since I was an awkward teenager myself). She excitedly told me that I should really try out the next time that they held try-outs. After the first talk with Janis, I was certainly enthused about my new school and the opportunities that would be afforded me at my new high school. I would be excited to see Janis at school each day and she was always friendly. She always tried to include me in conversations when she saw me.

About a week after school started I got the surprise of my life, Janis bicycled the three miles from her house over to say hello to me and visit with me; although at the time I was ashamed of my home; I felt so privileged to have a new friend like her. During the time that I went to school with Janis, Janis never forgot who I was or she was despite her tremendous popularity. She welcomed me to her home for parties and she even invited me to Bible Study in the music room before school. I have always treasured this special young lady. I know that I wasn't the only recipient of this gracious treatment.

THE MELODIES

I had just started to come into my own in the town of St. Francis, Minnesota when my father announced that we would be moving to Owatonna, Minnesota and that I would once again be embarking on a new school experience. This time however, I was a senior and extremely nervous about this move. I knew that I would love the town but I also was painfully shy.

God would intervene however with whom I lovingly refer to as the "Melodies" two wonderful teenage girls named Melody to make my final high school year more tolerable. The first Melody greeted me in French class and I was blessed to know that she too was a Christian girl and we had much in common. Her father was a minister of one of the local churches. Melody invited me to her church activities and we had a wonderful time together. She would later introduce me to more young ladies that became treasured friends.

The second Melody became a special friend in my time at high school because of her friendly and inclusive attitude, but in the years since high school has become extremely treasured. We had not seen each other for 10 years but our friendship was still as warm as it was in high school. Through the years Melody and I have become close. At first it was just Christmas cards at Christmas, but we still talk on the phone quite frequently and we enjoy getting to know each other better. Not too long ago we had a slumber party on the night of our high school reunion. In this high tech world of email and instant messaging, we have continued to keep the friendship going. I would hope that we all teach our children to be as kind to a new student at school or to that new person they meet along the way.

ETHEL AND CAROL

The first I remember meeting Carol and Ethel I knew that I had met friends for life. Ethel is my grandfather's cousin and lives in Texas. Her sister-in-law Carol lived a few blocks away from her. We were attending a family reunion and Ethel and Carol opened up their homes for the festivities. On the first night in Texas, Ethel brought about 20 of us into her home for dinner and then we all shared humorous stories about all of our growing years. Though I was the youngest of the whole group that first evening, they all listened to my stories with rapt attention and when it came time for the family sing along the next night, I was asked to sing a solo for the group. Ethel and Carol both accompanied me on the organ and piano. It was a wonderful treat that I never will forget.

The next time I met Carol and Ethel it was at Ethel's 50th anniversary celebration. Ethel and her husband Don had considered taking a cruise but had decided that they wanted their families to share in the event as well; so they rented several rooms at a very nice hotel in their town and basically paid our whole family's way. I remember the surprised look on my 15 year old daughter's face as each of these dear ladies hugged her and treated her special, introducing her to their own grandchildren so that she wouldn't be lonely.

The reason I put Ethel and Carol together is because I cannot imagine Ethel without her beloved sister-in-law Carol. They worked well together. They strived to make sure all of their guests are comfortable. On my last visit to Texas my mother and I stayed at Ethel's home. Due to weather conditions and traffic conditions from Oklahoma to their town, we were exceedingly late with our arrival, but Ethel was not perturbed, she welcomed us into her home despite the lateness of the hour and fed us and put us into their comfortable spare bedroom. The next morning before we left, Carol and her minister husband joined us for breakfast and they sent us off with a wonderful devotional and many hugs and a lifetime of memories. I am glad that I had the privilege of meeting these true Christian women. Since that trip, Carol has gone home to be with the Lord and Ethel is not at all well, but I will never forget their love and kindness.

The lesson I learned from these wonderful Christian ladies is that we are to treat all Christians like family. We are to be instant in season and out of season.

DORIS-ENTERTAINING STRANGERS

Several years ago I was traveling to Oregon via Colorado and my former husband, daughter and I were traveling by car. I remember that it was a very hot day, the scenery was beautiful however; with the mountains to the side of us as we drove and we happened to have car problems as we drove. It had taken us several hours to go only a few miles and we were hungry, thirsty and grimy. We managed to push our car into a small town on the eastern side of Grand Junction, Colorado.

We spotted a small Nazarene church on the edge of town with a few cars in the parking lot. As we pushed the car into the lot, we became aware that the service had just ended instead of just beginning. Disheartened we were not sure of what to do, but a kindly elderly gentleman came over to us, noticing our problem and he began to reassure us that they would be able to help us. If they were unable to get out car working that evening they would bring us to the church's mechanic the next morning. He piled our luggage into his car and we headed towards Grand Junction to find a "hotel".

It soon became clear that we would not be going to any ordinary hotel. It is at this point that we met "Doris" though this is not her real name, I am convinced that the Lord knows who she is and He would want us to tell everyone about her. When her husband drove us to his garage and parked the car with us in it in the garage, my husband and I both wondered what was going on. Doris' husband came back out and asked us if we would like to stay at their house. We were astounded. It was not normal in our neighborhood for people to take in people that they had never met. As we entered the house I can still see Doris usher us into her tidy, air-conditioned home. She asked us to be seated while she prepared what looked like the most sumptuous meal we had ever seen. She kept asking us if we wanted more and filling our plates saying, "Here, make with your supper". After we had eaten, she showed us the room that we would be sleeping in for the night and pointed out the shower (which we definitely needed). I should point out that this dear sweet woman had a rare form of cancer, so her health was in question, nonetheless she and her husband saw us on our way the next day and we were filled immense gratitude. Her kindness to us reminds me of the portion of the Bible that tells us not to hesitate to entertain strangers for we may be entertaining angels unaware. Though none of us are angels, I am certain that Doris and her dear husband were rewarded ten-fold for their kindness.

JEAN-ALMOST THE SHUMANITE WOMAN

I should not have been surprised that God works in mysterious ways with women because it had happened to me earlier in my life. I was living in Texas and was being evicted from the place I had been staying when members of a local Baptist church had come visiting. My friend with whom my two sons and I had been staying, drove me to the pastor's home The pastor was not at home but his wife was. When she learned that we were going to be on the street within two days, she arranged for my sons and I to stay with another woman from the church for the next night. She and her husband were making arrangements for where we would stay after that.

Little did I know that she would open up her own home to us for us to stay for six weeks in a room that had become a very special place to her. **Jean** will never know how much I truly appreciated her unselfishness at a time of her life when she was grieving the loss of her mother and suffering from debilitating illness, but I just had to share her story with others. Jean is now with the Lord and I think about her often. I was a rebellious young woman back then and not living for the Lord like I should, but Jean and her husband were faithful to God and were a real blessing to a young single mother with two small sons.

ELIZABETH-A HUG AND A CUP OF TEA

The first time that I met Elizabeth she gave me a hug. I had just met my future and now present husband and she welcomed me to her church. Elizabeth is just like that. Though neither of us still attend that particular church I can always count on Elizabeth to offer me a hot cup of tea and a hug when I'm feeling low. Elizabeth willingly shares her tea, her food and anything else the Lord allows her to have and I am thankful for her tender, kind hospitable spirit.

Sometimes hospitality isn't an easy thing to cultivate. When I was a young mother I longed to entertain people but found that I had little time to do so. Now that I am older and my children have grown I have learned that hospitality can be as small as making a phone call to a harried young mother, or perhaps an email of encouragement. Still better yet is a cup of tea in the middle of the day.

How has someone ministered to you with hospitality? In what ways did they share with you?

LIFE LESSONS IN THE WORKPLACE

"We all have different gifts according to the grace that God has given us."
Romans 12:6

SUPERVISORS EXTRAORDINAIRE

It seems that most of my time since I graduated from high school I have been working and I have learned much from each of my supervisors through the years. Some have been a positive influence in my life and some have not been as positive. Every one of us has at one time or another been encouraged or discouraged by those people who have had "rule" over us.

I remember vividly my first real job interview. After weeks of pounding the pavement looking for something that I would be good at but most importantly earn much needed money for secretarial school; I had reached a nonchalant attitude about obtaining employment.

My mother had pointed out an interesting position in the local newspaper and I had grudgingly gone to apply for it. I had been so certain that I would not get the position that I dressed in the most unprofessional outfit I had, a sundress and your basic flip-flops with no socks. I also had no experience in the business world, though I would be attending secretarial school in the fall, I had no basic training. I got the interview with the head of the human resource department that day; but more than that I met with **KARIN** the supervisor of the business office at the small hospital in Red Wing, Minnesota. I think that I knew I might be hired when they gave me my mantoux test which is required to work in any medical facility, but it hadn't sunk into my brain that I was actually hired until Monday, just two days later.

Karin gave me a chance to work as a cashier in the hospital business office working weekends, but she also saw that I desired to learn more than just what was required. By the time I left my position a year later, I had added switchboard operating and hospital admissions to my resume. Karin saw in me what I could not see. I may have been trying to defy my mother by the way I dressed but Karin saw the diamond somewhere in the coal. Karin has taught me not to look at the person's outside but to look at the possibilities. Although I had issues of immaturity, that basic trust cemented a grain of truth in me that I could do anything. Praise God for supervisors who see possibilities.

God has blessed me with several Christian managers through the years and some have shown extreme comfort and have also encouraged me to spread my wings and fly. **BETH** will always have a special place in my heart. She was another person whom I interviewed with and though I was positive that I would not get the job, it sounded ideal right from the start. They created a position within their clinic that was best suited for me, I was a radiology secretary. Through my employment at that company, I had the privilege of creating my whole position. Beth like Karin also trusted me to design my own position and consequently was used as a pattern for future radiology secretaries at that clinic. Beth was often supportive to me. During that time I went through many difficulties in my jobs. I had difficulty juggling the many roles that I was struggling to maintain in my life and Beth was supportive. Some women have difficulty meeting the high demands of child rearing and employment outside the home. It is extremely helpful when you have a boss who appreciates those demands. I was very blessed to have Beth as my friend as well as my boss. Beth often sent encouraging notes during the course of the time that I was in her employ.

Some employment opportunities in my life have not been positive ones for me. I remember a boss berating me in private and then threatening to terminate me if I said anything to anyone. From that employer I learned that sometimes God has other plans for us. Sometimes God teaches us that we need to live close to Him and trust Him to guide us through the immediate. I worked for a time for a temporary agency and I learned that the same thing applied. Sometimes the time would go by so fast and I would feel sad to see the position end and other times there would be a sense of relief. Temporary positions make you constantly aware of the brevity of a job and in correlation also help me to think about the fact that this world is not my home, I'm only passing through.

There has been a loss of many significant individuals in my life and it has been extremely encouraging to me to have supportive employers. The department that I worked for had had major transition in the years while I was employed there. We had several supervisors in our department and I have treasured each one. When one of my last supervisors transferred to another department I remember weeping about her leaving and she promised that I would absolutely love my new boss. I was pretty cynical about the person who would replace her. I could not imagine anyone being that good but I was surprised when I met **WENDY**.

Wendy's professional, yet warm personality was the first thing that I noticed. She came into our department and within the first week had already discovered areas of improvement in our department. She was also extremely intuitive in discovering each person's strengths. I was also encouraged to know that Wendy was a Christian. From the first day, I was thrilled to know that Wendy wanted to make our department the best of the best. She did a tremendous job of turning our once dysfunctional department into a more harmonious one. She challenged me to become more than just a mediocre employee and helped me to see who I am in Christ and just exactly what He wants me to be. I am thankful for this dynamo entering my life and I know that should though God changed our positions that He knows what is best.

WONDERFUL CO-WORKERS

God has not only taught me through employers but also the co-workers I have been blessed to work with. One of my most precious memories of co-workers is the blessed time that I had at a bank that I worked at. Someone had started a Bible Study on Tuesday mornings and this was a very special time. It helped us pray as one for the needs of our office staff who were not Christians and it was helpful to pray for other needs. One of the women at this time was going through an extremely difficult time. She was pregnant with her first child and her husband was dying of cancer. We prayed earnestly for her husband but the Lord allowed him to be taken home and **CATHY** was left alone. She soon gave birth to a beautiful little girl and we all continued to pray for God's strength during her trials. Imagine my surprise when Cathy came by my desk one day and told me that she had heard I had a baby and she had something for me. I was touched. Here was I praying for Cathy and God had laid me on her heart. I lost touch with Cathy but I still remember with joy the beautiful gesture of love that she showed to me.

SUSAN

I had mentioned my working as a temporary employee and the joys of having short-term jobs. I have been so blessed with co-workers at each one that either were Christian or just really good people. At most of the places that I worked it was difficult for me to leave each place. One clinic that I worked for I was their switchboard operator for 5 ½ months so I had become almost part of their staff. In fact, I strongly considered working for their group but God had other plans. That time was probably one of the most stressful times of my life. My grandmother had been diagnosed months before with colon cancer; and during my last week of working at that particular clinic we learned that the chemo therapy had not worked and the family was aware that my grandmother would be going home to be with the Lord very soon.

During this time I got to know a nurse by the name of **SUSAN** whose own mother was battling cancer. I remember the day I learned that the cancer had attacked the liver and that it would only be a matter of time before Grandma would be gone. Susan held me while I cried and let me talk things out. Most of the people at that clinic had been extremely comforting when Grandma died just 4 days later but Susan had taken the time to just let me work through the grief and I hope that I was able to encourage her and help her during her time as well. She will never know the debt of gratitude that I owe to her.

God blessed me currently with Christian coworkers. One of these dear ladies has been such an encouragement to me. I have seen **DIANA** blossom and grow since I began working with her. She became an encourager to me. I know that I have been so blessed to have her as my friend. Recently she was concerned for my spiritual well being and gave me a book for growth. I am in awe that she would take the time to pray for me and especially for my spiritual needs. When you work with Christians and they actually live out their faith it can make your day worthwhile. I know that I work with other people that are not as outspoken about their faith, but I am so thankful for Diana's not being afraid to share her faith with others.

I thank God for all of the people He has brought to my path at work both the good and the bad. These have all been a learning experience for me. My prayer is that I might be that encouragement to people that I work with. That I might not always be the recipient of goodness but that I would expel goodness in my actions toward my co-workers.

People spend a lot of time at work. Who has touched your life? Can you think of ways that you might touch a co-worker's life?

HAPPILLY EVER SINGLE

"Whatever you have learned or received from me put into practice." Phillipians 4:9

When I was a young girl my greatest desire was to be married and have children. That is what I thought my mission in life was to be. I am sure that many young ladies grow up with those same dreams and goals. The women that I will mention in this section had those goals also but for some reason have never married, never had children but have been used by God in wonderful ways.

DEBORAH

If you were to talk to Deborah, I am sure that she would be the first to tell you that it was never her intention to be single. She was attractive and had a good career and loved children. This was evidenced by the career that she decided upon. She, like most women enjoyed companionship with men but as the years have progressed, she has developed a closer relationship with God. She speaks proudly of her many nieces and nephews and of the students she has taught through the years.

Deborah has a sweet spirit and is an asset in her church family. She has raised many Christian young men and women through the years; influencing far more than she would had she been a mother. In essence, teachers do become second parents to children. I remember my children calling their teacher mom as I must confess, so did I. Deborah was also able to travel to far away lands that she might not have had she married. This unclaimed blessing has accomplished far more than she would if she were distracted by the requirements of marriage and family. I applaud her for her accomplishments and I know that when her true "Bridegroom" comes for her, she will be ready for Him to take her to Heaven to be with Him.

DIANE

I have known Diane since I was a young girl. We grew up in the same youth group for several years. The average teenager probably wouldn't have noticed Diane on the street. She was not popular and did not have many friends and yet she considered me to be one of them. Looking back I consider it a high honor that she did but I don't think I was the kind of friend I should have been.

Diane was slightly different from the rest of the youth group. Whenever something needed to be done as far as labor in the church, Diane was one of the first people thought of to help and she never complained. While many of the girls in our youth group were dating, Diane did not, she opted instead to stay home and to help her mother with projects there. Diane loved to sing. She mostly loved to sing praises to God and it was about this time that I was paired up with Diane because our voices blended well. When you are a teenager, you want desperately to fit in and I certainly wanted that. I am sure Diane wanted that too.

Diane grew up and desired the same thing that all young girls wish for. She too wanted a husband and a family. That was never to be, however. Diane, like our other young woman filled her life with hard work and singing. Diane was not an accomplished singer but she still enjoyed singing praises to God in hymns and choruses.

Diane was stricken with breast cancer. Diane could have filled her life with "poor me" but she did not do that. She met this challenge with dignity and joy. She filled her days with supporting those people she came into contact with in the nursing home she lived in. She also filled her days making other people happier. I cannot think of a greater joy than knowing what God wants you to do and doing it. It seems to me that being single helped Diane to keep that in perspective.

MANDY

There are some unclaimed blessings that don't realize just what a blessing they are to those around them. Mandy was one of those women. Mandy grew up desiring the same things that most young girls did. She wanted a husband and a family. She was a pretty young woman with the voice of an angel. Mandy was one of those young women who made friends with men easily, often becoming a confidante and encourager to them, but as some men are, they dismissed Mandy for one reason or another from being a prospective wife.

Mandy was a talented singer and musician, singing often in her church; however, soon she became well known in her community for doing outdoor concerts and singing in local funerals. Still, Mandy desired more. She still wanted to have a family and she wanted to record an album of Contemporary Christian music and be recognized by the world. After a few years, Mandy collaborated on an album with a friend and they distributed it to several churches and friends in her town.

Mandy continued with the hope that she would still find someone to love and have her own children and then the crushing blow came. Mandy was still fairly young when the doctor told her that she would have to have a complete hysterectomy. Mandy was devastated. This wasn't fair. She had seen all but one of her siblings give birth to at least one child but she was to be denied? Why? What had she done wrong? Mandy tried to trust in the Lord, knowing that He makes no mistakes but it was hard. She still had her music and her health for the most part and then IT happened. Mandy fell and broke her foot. She continued to go through surgery after surgery with no healing. She still continued to wonder why. It was obvious to her that she would never have a husband or a family now. And then it dawned on her. As a single woman, she was able to travel easier and to relieve her siblings when they needed respite from their children. She could be there for them. Though it wasn't an ideal thought, she was in essence a mother and could be an encourager to her nieces and nephew like no one else could and they in turn developed a bond with her.

I remember my last visit with Mandy. She had just sung in her church, a stirring rendition of "I'd Rather Have Jesus" and she seemed content. She wasn't as concerned anymore that the man she had loved for many years hastily married someone else. She was trying desperately to dwell on her "husband" God. Mandy wasn't perfect and she knew that she had shortcomings but she was so in tune to making the most of the time God had given her.

Mandy's foot developed a sudden foot infection and Mandy was confined to a hospital where she died. At last, Mandy had met her bridegroom.

OLIVE

Although I was pretty young while Olive was alive, I heard many stories about her as I was growing up. Olive grew up in Wisconsin and was a single woman her whole life, yet I would be remiss if I didn't share about her. Olive was one of the many daughters born to my great-great grandparents and I learned that she was a very able woman who I believe exuded courage and security.

Olive took the initiative in a man's world to begin her own bakery in the town she lived in. Her bakery goods were the best for miles around people would say. She often employed her younger nieces and nephews and I am told that she was an excellent employer. Olive was an independent woman who cared about her family, often sending money to her nieces and nephews when she suspected that they needed it. Though she was not wealthy or in the best of health, Olive was a comfortable woman and took care of her younger sister who had always been sickly and made provision for her for when she died. The lesson I learned from Olive is that although she may have wanted to be married, Olive was a Christian woman who was not dependent on a man to take care of her. She was doing what she could with what God had blessed her with, and she was blessed beyond measure.

BRENDA

I went to high school and college with. Through the years I had known that this lovely woman had never married, that God had for some reason allowed her to remain single. I recently learned that she has gone on to become a nurse, obtain her masters degree and has become a nurse practitioner. I am amazed at her positive spirit. Like Olive, and many of the other women I have shared about, Brenda's faith and trust has sustained her. I do not believe that we are just born with the positive attitude. It is something that we grown in like our Christian faith.

There are countless women that I have met through the years that God has allowed singleness to remain. I have held many young women who wept bitterly that God had not allowed them to marry. I have often felt the same way. In I Corinthians it says that though marriage is a good thing that it is also a good thing to remain unmarried. I wish we could teach little girls that although being married to a man is important, how much more important it is to have that relationship with our Lord and Savior. He is truly where our hearts should be.

Has God brought any single women to you have been encouraged by? What lessons have they taught you regarding being single?

ENCOURAGERS ALONG THE WAY

"Charm is deceitful and beauty is vain but a woman who fears the Lord will be praised." Proverbs 31:3

God gives many people many different gifts and one of the gifts that I am thankful for is the gift of encouragement. God has blessed me with many Christian sisters who have that gift. I would be honored to share their stories of encouragement with you.

MARJORIE

The first moment you meet Marjorie you know that she not only has the gift of hospitality but she has the gift of encouragement. Marjorie often sends notes of uplift to sick people in our Sunday school class and to needy people. There have been countless times that she has sent me notes of cheer or maybe even dropped a small bill in the mail and I know that she cheers many others in the same manner. Marjorie's nurturing spirit can be felt and she has been a definite encourager to me.

MYRNA

Myrna is a very special lady who attends my former church. Myrna has had rheumatoid arthritis for several years and is in very poor health, but Myrna has taken it on herself to be an encouragement to others. Myrna writes greeting cards to her whole church family and often makes phone calls to encourage lonely people. On Sundays her husband and her pick up several senior citizens and bring them to church. People who would not normally have an opportunity to get out to church get a ride from Myrna and her husband. The lesson that I learn from Myrna is that a person doesn't have to have perfect health to minister for the Lord. I pray that I have the courage to minister in such a loving way.

NONIE

Nonie grew up on the mission field in Pakistan and is a very active woman in my church's women's ministries. I can always count on Nonie to send me a warm note of encouragement. When my daughter was going through a difficult time, she sent her many warm notes and for that I am grateful.

HARRIET

My youngest son joined the military a few years back and Harriet became a special friend to me. As time has passed, I have appreciated her willingness to pray for me and not just try to "fix" my problems but actually listen to them. She and her husband took me under their wing for some needs that I had and I want to say that this has been extremely touching during tough times. I consider Harriet closer than a sister and am so thankful to have her shape me up when I need it.

MARIE

I met Marie shortly after I began going to my church. Marie was active in our Sunday school class as a coordinator of sorts for our Shepherd's ministry. Marie organizes many things for people who are in need in our church. A few years back when my house burned and I moved to my new home, Marie coordinated several women to help me unpack boxes, put things away and so forth to help me be comfortable. Many brought goodies for me and made me feel welcome. Later that year when I had foot surgery, Marie arranged for several women to bring meals to me for a couple of weeks afterward.

Marie also helps to organize many other ministries. She calls several people when they have been away for several weeks. She arranges for various people in need and she gives rides to church for people who don't have one. I think that God has blessed Marie with such a wonderful gift of encouragement and caring.

Has God blessed you with encouragers in your life that you can count on when you need them? If so, what have you learned from them? In what way can you show encouragement to others around you?

SOMETIMES IT'S HARD TO STAND BY YOUR MAN

"But if your first concern is to look after yourself, you will never find yourself. But if you forget about yourself and look to Me; you'll find both yourself and Me. **Matt 10:39**

The book of First Peter is an extreme encouragement to women who have the unfortunate position of being married to non-believers. The Apostle Peter tells women to reverence their husbands and to strive to be a loving wife so that their unsaved spouse might be won through their testimony. The women I have chosen to highlight in this portion are women that I believe fit Peter's description to a tee. Though they are imperfect, their faithfulness to their spouses and their Lord are an eye opener to all women and an encouragement to those in similar circumstances.

HARRIET

Harriet has been a Christian for numerous years and has been active in her church for the same amount of time. She and her husband were married for over 60 years. When I first met Harriet over 30 years ago, I was a teenager she was praying for her husband to accept Christ. He was a good man, a kind man, but he did not know Him.

Harriet prayed long and hard those days as her children were growing up and she tried to walk circumspectly around them. I never heard her say an unkind word about her spouse or her situation though I knew that it was a burden that she often felt like she was carrying it alone.

Her husband was watching her testimony and also watching those around him, looking for answers and wanting to see authenticity in their steps. Harriet was diligent though those around her were not as faithful.

Harriet's faithfulness was not unseen. Her husband eventually accepted Christ and they attended church together until she went home to be with the Lord. It took many long years of faithful praying and following Christ, but her continued modeling paid off.

MARION

Marion was 24 when she met Alvin and decided to marry him. In the community she had grown up in, women had married at an earlier age. Although Alvin would be a good provider, Marion's family knew that Alvin did not profess a faith in Christ and that was a very important factor to be decided in her marriage.

Marion was not to be dissuaded from her decision and so the two were united. As time went on, Marion discovered that her husband was extremely abusive and a drinker; still, Marion stayed true to her vows and her faith. When Marion's second to the youngest child passed away, Marion stoically stood by and trusted God to get her through though it was difficult and even more difficult was to continue to be faithful to Alvin who's disposition never seemed to change. 60 years passed and during that time, Marion saw the death of two more grown children as well as the loss of her parents. It seemed to Marion that Alvin's heart seemed to be hardened to the gospel and to people of her church family. It was hardened that is; until Marion was stricken with stomach cancer. Alvin saw again Marion's faithfulness to her God and saw her take her final walk faithfully with little complaining and dignity.

Alvin saw what he had seen for over 65 years; he saw a faithful, loving wife and he saw that she never wavered from her belief and it pricked his heart. Alvin realized that he was a sinner and that only by accepting the fact that God sent His only son to die on the cross for his sins, could Alvin realize salvation. Alvin made that profession of faith months after Marion's death. He had plenty of time to contemplate and remember her testimony as he had never before. Less than a year after Marion died, Alvin too passed on believing that the Lord had redeemed him and that he would see his faithful wife in Heaven.

I am reminded of the verse that reads "They who sow in tears shall reap in joy." Though Marion did not see the results on earth, I believe she sees that result in Heaven now.

Consider also, **MARYANN** married for many years to an abusive husband. She endured several years of inflicted abuse from her spouse never imagining anything different. She faithfully served her husband and raised their four children. When God allowed him to pass away, several years later MaryAnn met a man who treasured her and cared for her and she remarried and had several good years to this wonderful man.

ARLYN was also a woman who stood by her husband until the day her abusive spouse died. She had 11 children with this man and I am sure that there were days that she felt like giving up but she hung in there. I remember her children telling me about those tough times growing up and that their mother rarely complained, even though she was forced to adopt out at least one of her children. Though I do not necessarily agree with staying with an abusive spouse, Arlyn's long-suffering spirit is one that will remain with me forever.

Can you think of women whose lives have touched yours whose testimony stood out to those around them as well as their husbands?

SHORT TERM FRIENDSHIPS THAT LAST FOREVER

**"The joy of the Lord is your strength."
Nehemiah 8:10**

Every now and then there are people that come into our lives for brief moments. They change our lives and then they are gone. I have met several young ladies that have taught me many lessons. Some have taught joy in the journey, others have taught acceptance and still others have taught me to have faith in the tough times.

TIFFANY

The first time I saw Tiffany, I wasn't sure that I wanted to know Tiffany. She appeared to be just your typical teenager. She was energetic and had a real enjoyment of singing. And my teenage son was totally enthralled with her. I soon realized that Tiffany was anything but a typical teenager. She was a girl with a tender heart and a desire to be loved. Tiffany's parents had divorced a while before I met her and Tiffany was living with her paternal grandparents and her father. Tiffany came regularly to youth activities and always seemed pretty upbeat not alluding to the inner turmoil that was going on around her.

In ensuing weeks I would discover that Tiffany had been fighting cancer since she was nine years of age and at the age of 16 it was presumably gone. Tiffany spoke easily to anyone that would talk with her. She was so hungry for a good "mom" role model. Up until that point I was pretty uninvolved in Tiffany's life and for some reason God impressed upon me to open myself up to her. Sometimes like all teenage girls, she exasperated me, and yet at other times she tugged at my heart. I remember vividly the day that she shared with me that she was out of remission. My dear grandmother had just passed and I still found it difficult to say the word **CANCER**. When she asked me to break the news to my children I was frightened. This was not something I was happy to do. I can still see my son's angry face as I broke the news and his angry weeping. He had dated Tiffany briefly but still in his heart I think he had hoped that she was the one.

The therapy treatments began and Tiffany was getting weary. I remember going to see her at her grandmother's house hoping to cheer her up and yet I was the one who walked away blessed. One of Tiffany's goals was to graduate high school and to go to Alaska. Thankfully she got to do both.

Tiffany has been gone for many years now and she is deeply missed by all that knew her. The biggest lesson I learned is that you cannot judge a book by its cover. Tiffany proved that time and again and taught me that God is faithful and accepts us wherever we are at. We need only to accept Him.

PAT

I could never forget one of the best teachers that I ever met in my life. Pat was an encouragement to me from the first time this gangly, shy teenager entered the high school she taught at. From the first time I met her, she made me feel as though she really cared about me as her student. She saw possibility in me that I could not see in myself. I had a penchant for drama in elementary and junior high but few people thought that I had a talent. Pat encouraged me not only to try out for the plays, but she surprised me when she selected me to be her student director for our fall play. She allowed me latitude to not only help direct but also recognized that I had a knack for memorizing the parts of our cast members.

She then encouraged me to try out for the speech team that she also coached and I actually went as far as the state for competition. Pat became a special friend long after high school though we rarely see one another except in passing in a grocery store or whatnot, but ironically she taught my daughter in 10th grade English class as well. I am thankful for teachers like Pat who take the time to see a special quality in their students and who see them as more than students, but they see them as people. Though my acting career never advanced beyond college, I still thank Pat for giving me a chance to express myself in acting as well as in speech.

SARAH

I don't know of a grandmother alive who doesn't think her grandchildren are the most beautiful, precious gift they have ever seen. Though she is not a woman (and won't be for a long time), I wanted to share some lessons about this wonderful little one. To me, Sarah has been a balm to soothe the troubled soul. My granddaughter Sarah was born on my birthday of my 45th year. I had been dreading grandparenthood fiercely. Certainly this was not a planned pregnancy, but the baby that was born was angelic (I'm not biased) and has taught me a lot about the circle of life. Babies are amazing little people. They come into this world small and fragile and before you know it they have you wrapped around their little finger. I am noticing Sarah's distinct little personality shining through. Her little smile brightens up even my darkest day and I love how little people trust adults. She does not have distrust built into her yet like some adults do. Since I have begun writing this; Sarah asked me to lead her to Christ, an honor I have been humbled to have.

BONNIE

A few years back, my grandparents, my mother and I attended a family reunion in Bryan, Texas at Valentine's time. It was a wonderful family time. Bonnie was one of my grandfather's cousins and we had an enjoyable time getting to know each other. I remember her handing a book about her life in missions to each major family member and I remember her excitement as she shared about all of the various mission fields that God had allowed her to work.

The thing that still sticks in my mind about Bonnie is that though I had never met her before she took the time to get to know me. On that side of my grandfather's family we enjoy singing great hymns of the faith and telling our stories about faith. Bonnie shared her stories with us. She kept us laughing and smiling. Looking back on the opportunity, had my family not shared her secret with me, I might have thought that it would always be like that.

It was evident though, that Bonnie was sick. In fact more sick than she would let on to those around her. She had leukemia and was dying. We would not have known it had she not in private shared with us how low her white blood count was. She had been fighting this disease for a long time and she was tired. I can still see her fighting spirit as she hugged us all goodbye and sent us on our way back to Minnesota. I couldn't wait to read her book that she had written. It was hard to put down. I realized what she was doing, she was sharing her love for missions with us with the hope that someone would carry on and take up the slack that she would leave behind and she did leave behind a large gap. For me, it was a challenge to not be afraid to go out of my comfort zone for the Lord. Praise the Lord for this wonderful, Godly woman.

Reality series' have become a staple in the television world and I have for the most part avoided these programs, however, one program grabbed my attention so much so that I decided to try out for this program. I realized that my chances of being chosen for this program were next to impossible; nevertheless, I drove the 500 miles to Chicago to try out. God had a plan for why I drove all that way just for a 5-minute interview. I learned that God had more important things in mind when He allowed me to meet some wonderful Christian ladies that I doubt that I will ever see again on this side of Glory, but I wanted to share them with you. The first woman I want to share with you is **DONNA**. Donna is a recently divorced woman with grown children. Donna's effervescent smile first caught my eye and we began to share our faith in God with one another. Talk about a God thing. This definitely was one. Donna easily shared the sadness of learning of her husband's betrayal with her best friend and then she shared about her growth since her divorce. The lesson I learned from Donna is that although we may be miles apart, each of us has our share of sorrows, however, it's how we cope with these sorrows that sets us apart. Life is a journey and we are given tools for the journey. How do we use those tools in that journey?

Another dear lady that I met that same weekend was **DIANE**. Diane was also looking for a way to cope with her dilemmas in life. Recently widowed, this lovely woman was still grieving the loss of her dear husband five months earlier and was grieving the loss of stillborn twins. I am thankful God allowed that meeting that day. Donna, Diane, my sister-in-law and I shared a wonderful lunch over pizza and we laughed and cried and hugged. Sometimes it's those "chance" meetings that teach us the most about life. We think that we are going for one reason and God orchestrates another plan.

Family has always been important to me but it was not until 1999 that I had the privilege of getting to know many of my grandfather's cousins and their families. Though I had always valued my immediate family, I had never researched or met his family and I learned many things during that weekend that I discussed in an earlier portion of my book.

During that weekend I learned about the strength of many of my ancestors and of their children and I desire to share some of those things with you. My grandfather's mother was one of several daughters born to my great-great grandfather and it was this man and his daughters we were honoring. During the course of that weekend I had the delightful opportunity to "interview" many of my cousins and learn of their faith. I have already introduced you to Ethel and her sister-in-law Carol. I told you about Bonnie and her desire to reach out and meet all of her family members and to give them peace of mind before she said her final farewell. I would like to share more of the lessons I learned.

GENEVA'S mother had passed away when she was at an early age and she did not have the opportunity to get to know her as well as she wanted to but she has blossomed and developed in her own way. In her interview with me she shared about all of the joys in her life. "I have had a wonderful life," she shared, "I have seen so much. I have traveled all over the world, I have had a wonderful husband and great children." Although she had been left motherless at an early age, she was not complaining the fact that she had not had a mother but rather she was counting the blessings that God had given her. She excitedly told me about her experience of traveling to the Holy Land and meeting the King of Jordan when she was a younger woman. She had encouraged her son to become a singer and he had recorded a hit single. A few months later, I reflected my conversation with Geneva as I learned that she had cancer of the mouth and has had to endure numerous surgeries and treatments and though she is no longer the vivacious older woman that I met, her spirit still shines through.

Each of us encounters people for a short time. Who in your life has impacted you in the short time that you have known them?

STANDING BY MY MAN ALL THE WAY

"Every good gift and every perfect gift is from above." James 1:17.

Keeping a marriage strong has always been difficult and the twenty-first century is no exception. Because we are all imperfect creatures, the desire to be in charge has always been a struggle in relationships. I am unfortunately one of those statistics that you read about in studies. My heart is warmed, however when I read of marriages that have withstood the test of time.

KAY

I am reminded of one of my dear friends who stood by her husband even at a time when most women would have given up on them. I will not go into details because that's not the important thing, but Kay has proven to be the strong, patient woman of God that He would have us all to be. Her marriage is stronger than ever because of this and she is radiant.

RUTH

My Aunt Ruth is also a stellar example of a woman who stands by her man. My uncle is a minister and she has willingly followed my uncle for over almost 50 years as he has begun new church works in various parts of the country. They have lived in Pennsylvania and begun churches in Florida as well as Colorado and California.

I know that times have not always been flourishing and that they have seen many lean years, but I am impressed with the support and love that she has shown her husband all these years. She has not only loved him, but she has been gracious and kind to many in need. She works long hours to supplement their income by doing in-home health care. She has never wavered from her vows and has been a strong example to her five grown children and her grandchildren.

Think of women that you know that have shown strong support to their spouses especially during trying times in their marriages. What was their attitude during those times?

LORD, IT'S HARD TO BE HUMBLE

"Your attitude should be the same as that of Jesus Christ." Phillipians 2:5

One of the most horrifying times in our American history in recent memory has to have been the shootings at Columbine High School in Colorado. I have heard that many hearts were touched after the shooting and God worked in many lives.

I remember about a week after the shootings that I received a long-distance phone call from my former in-laws in the middle of the day. I envisioned something horrible having happened to my children's father or something. I wasn't prepared for the tearful voices that greeted me. Immediately they shared that they had just been to Columbine.

MARGARET, my former mother-in-law spoke first earnestly begging my forgiveness for all wrongs that she might have done to me during the time that I was married to her son and in the time since (which was about 15 years or more). I realized how humiliating it must have been for her to humble herself and I was touched. What a commentary for a woman to humble herself and apologize. Sorry to say that I have not always gone to those I have hurt but I was encouraged to do so that day. As women of God, can you imagine how free we would be if we actively sought restitution and forgiveness from our Christian brothers and sisters? I have a feeling that I will never forget that turning point in my relationship with Margaret even though she was stricken with Alzheimer's disease and gone to be with the Father, I am thankful that on a sunny day in April Margaret took the time to call me.

Who is the first woman that comes to your mind when you think about a humble, forgiving spirit? Why do you think she is this way?

THINGS DIDN'T GO THE WAY I PLANNED THEM

"If we confess our sins He is faithful and just to forgive us." I John 1:9

RACHEL

After two rambunctious sons God blessed me with a beautiful daughter. **RACHEL** has taught me many lessons as she has grown up. I was in uncharted waters when Rachel was born. I was a divorced mom trying to make ends meet and I was also trying to be a good mommy to my children. Rachel and I have often had a tumultuous relationship. As puberty hit, I realized that I was in over my head. I did not always make wise decisions when it came to rearing her. I know that many times I thought that I was being fair but she did not think so. It was extremely difficult for Rachel to grow up in a home without her biological father and I know she was disappointed that her stepfather did not understand her.

When she was little. Rachel made a profession of faith. Unfortunately the teenage years are tough on adolescents. Needless to say, Rachel gave birth to my granddaughter when she was young and married Sarah's father. They now have three small children. I know that the road Rachel travels is not an easy one, but the lesson I have learned from her is perseverance in adversity. Sometimes the decisions we make are not what others would make, but we ultimately are responsible for our decisions and ultimately we answer to God for all we do. She has also taught me patience. My prayer for my only daughter and all my children is that they would let God use them to be who He wants them to be.

Surrender is the hardest isn't it? If you had asked me a while back if I would be comfortable in what God has for me to do I would have answered a resounding no! Circumstances had bogged me down and I was overwhelmed. As I surrender my wants, wishes and desires to God, I am amazed at how close to God I am; if I choose however to ignore God's promptings I have more problems than I can wish to deal with.

It has been said that each person on this earth impacts approximately 250 people in their lifetime. My purpose of this book has been to share my stories with you, but on a more personal level, how have you impacted other people? I know that when I meet my Father in Heaven that I want to know that I have served Him well and that I have been a witness for Him.

In what ways do you think that you impact others in your life? How do you think God wants to use you?

LaVergne, TN USA
04 December 2009
165966LV00002B/51/P